Praise for The Crisis of Our T

Rational self-interest is the American Dream. The cruel irony is that as Americans in general have modeled themselves in this image, they charge toward their own destruction. In *The Crisis of Our Time*, Morris Berman gives a fascinating account of how we are not only no longer able to understand ourselves through stories and poetry but are also cut off from our own bodies--a kind of cultural dementia. The rational human globule has become sick, stunted, and unable to cope with climate change, the pathology of artificial intelligence, and the multitudes of other maladies crashing around us. Yet Berman sees a backlash on the horizon as the younger generation is becoming more cognizant that the American Dream is actually a nightmare, from which they are beginning to awaken.

This book is a fabulous addition to Berman's collection of essays on American culture and is an inspiration for authentic creative thinking about our future.

—Joel Magnuson is an economist and author of several books, the most recent of which is *The Dharma and Socially Engaged Buddhist Economics* (2022).

Also By Morris Berman

Social Change and Scientific Organization

TRILOGY ON HUMAN CONSCIOUSNESS:

The Reenchantment of the World

Coming to Our Senses

Wandering God: A Study in Nomadic Spirituality

TRILOGY ON THE AMERICAN EMPIRE:

The Twilight of American Culture

Dark Ages America: The Final Phase of Empire

Why America Failed: The Roots of Imperial Decline

A Question of Values (essays)

Destiny (fiction)

Counting Blessings (poetry)

Spinning Straw Into Gold (memoir)

The Man Without Qualities (fiction)

Are We There Yet? (essays)

Neurotic Beauty: An Outsider Looks at Japan

Genio: The Story of Italian Genius

The Heart of the Matter (fiction)

Eminent Post-Victorians

Healing: The Defining Root of Our Existence

The Soul of Russia

The Crisis of our Time

Morris Berman

Copyright © 2024 by Morris Berman

All rights reserved.

ISBN: 9798877536098

"Ithaka" from *C. P. CAVAFY: Collected Poems*, Revised Edition translated by Edmund Keeley and Philip Sherrard, ed. by George Savidis. Translation copyright © 1975, 1992 by Edmund Keeley and Philip Sherrard. Reprinted by permission of Princeton University Press via Copyright Clearance Center.

Also, thanks go to:

Hildan Ammar for the sketches of Pirsig, Cavafy, Parry, and Turing.

Shutterstock for the cover artwork.

Azucena Guerra for the author's photo.

Jeffrey P. Fisher for layout and design.

However intoxicating the attractions of intellect and however essential to the structures by which we live, something in us wants also the clear signal of the senses by which alone the world is made fresh and definite.

—J.H. Finley, *Four Stages of Greek Thought*

Contents

Introduction	xi
1. The Oral-Poetic Tradition	1
2. The Physicality of Aesop	17
3. Lives of Quiet Desperation	23
4. Backlash	31
Notes	53
About the Author	59

Introduction
Rethinking Pirsig, Fifty Years On

[W]hat we need is not to abandon reason, but simply to recognise that reason in the last three centuries has worked within a field which is not the whole of experience, [and] that it has mistaken the part for the whole.

—L.C. Knights, *Explorations* (1946)

Quality! Virtue! Dharma! That is what the Sophists were teaching! *Not* ethical relativism. *Not* pristine "virtue." But *areté*. Excellence. *Dharma!* Before the Church of Reason. Before substance. Before form. Before mind and matter. Before dialectic itself. Quality had been absolute. Those first teachers of the Western world were teaching *Quality*, and the medium they had chosen was that of rhetoric.

INTRODUCTION

—Robert Pirsig, *Zen and the Art of Motorcycle Maintenance*

This book—my book—could have had an alternative, if unwieldy, title: How Did Robert Pirsig's *Zen and the Art of Motorcycle Maintenance* Manage to Sell Five Million Copies? It has been called the most popular, and influential, philosophy book ever written. The literary critic George Steiner, a man not given to lavish praise, compared it to *Moby-Dick* in importance. Published in 1974, this autobiographical novel remained near the top of the best-seller lists for a decade. How in the world did this happen?

Asked about the huge, unexpected success of *Zen*, Pirsig replied by characterizing it as a "culture-bearing book." Such a book, he went on, doesn't change the culture; rather, it heralds a change already underway. I was simply expressing my own thoughts, he said, "and they turned out to be the prime thoughts of everybody else."

And that really is the key to it. Dissatisfaction with Western culture, in particular with the dominance of science and rationality over that culture, was in the air during the 1960s, with Herbert Marcuse's *One-Dimensional Man* (1964) and culminating in Theodore Roszak's *Making of a Counter Culture* (1969)—also a culture-bearer. *Zen's* timing couldn't have been better; it hit a nerve that had been pulsating for some time: the notion that there was something fundamentally wrong with our (Western industrial) way of life. That percep-

Introduction

tion is still with us, and in my opinion, at least, is quite accurate. But it is hardly a great intellectual breakthrough, at this point, to declare that things have turned out badly for us, and have seriously gone awry. Fifty years after Pirsig, it might be time to re-open his argument, and take a closer look at it. Exactly what was he saying?(1)

Robert Pirsig

The ghost of Nietzsche hangs over Pirsig's book, in particular the assertion that with Socrates and Plato, Western philosophy took a wrong turn. In *The Birth of Tragedy*, Nietzsche claimed that Socrates was "the herald of a radically dissimilar culture" to the one that prevailed in ancient Greece—what I call the (Homeric) oral-poetic tradition, which was grounded in instinct and intuition. (See Chapter 1.) Socrates, says Nietzsche, had "a corrosive influence upon instinctual life." He sought to replace this mode with reason, rationality, and to extend this theoretical approach to knowledge to the entire world. As a result, "we cannot help viewing Socrates as the vortex and turning point of Western civilization." Our present age, he concludes, is "the result of a Socratism bent on the extermination of myth." This loss, he maintains, has left us in desperate straits. Our culture is one that "no matter how much it consumes, remains insatiable." As H.G. Wells so succinctly put it, the Western mind is at the end of its tether. Western life as well.(2)

All this is why, in the famous words of Alfred North Whitehead, Western philosophy can be summarized as "a series of footnotes to Plato." Plato's promise of rational clarity subsequently merged into Christianity; a vision, says the Harvard classicist J.H. Finley, that lasted for 1,500 years (more, actually). This, he concludes, was Plato's mission, and his victory. "Plato and Aristotle wanted a conceptual clarity and much in our civilization follows from their choice," writes Finley; "but to Homer this clarity of the mind came second to the clarity of the senses." As for Pirsig, his mission in life was to try to reverse all of that, in particular by resurrecting the world view and reputation of Socrates' opponents (according to Pirsig), the Sophists, who argued for rhetoric over reason. "Our current modes of rationality are not moving society forward into a better world.... [Rationality] begins to be seen for what it really is— emotionally hollow, esthetically meaningless and spiritually empty." If Plato was victorious, Pirsig was not; and in the process of his war on reason, managed to go insane. Yet the jury is still out; he may, after all, have the last laugh.(3)

Zen and the Art of Motorcycle Maintenance describes a trip Pirsig made across the country on a motorbike in 1968 in the aftermath of all that, with his son Chris, who was eleven years old at the time. It is more of an interior, psychological trip than a physical one, as Pirsig now has time to reflect on what happened to him. Who am I? is the question, and What do I believe now? What *did* happen in ancient Greece, and how did this manage to create the disaster that is contemporary America, and modern life in general? This is the subject of the book, and of his trip across the United States.

Pirsig's answer is epitomized by the epigraph to this chapter, which is the baldest and most direct statement of the entire book: the argument that reason destroyed what he calls "Quality." It will be important to take a close look at this statement, and identify the problems with it.

- Problem No. 1: Pirsig never defines "Quality." In fact, he says it can't be defined, only intuited, which could understandably leave his readers at a loss. Nevertheless, my own feeling is that he was onto something; that there may be some truth to this, the idea that a belief or assertion could be subjectively true.

- No. 2: Dharma is a concept found in Indian religions, and has multiple meanings. One meaning is virtue, or "the right way of living." But it is certainly not a Western concept, and it is rather a stretch to say this was what the Sophists were teaching. (Not a total stretch, however; again, Pirsig was partially correct.)
- No. 3: The Sophists were, in fact, ethical relativists. "Man is the measure of all things," their most famous phrase, meant that the truth was subjective; there was no absolute truth. Rather, they claimed, it depended on who was speaking.
- No. 4: The Sophists were not the first teachers in the West; the Pythagoreans, who emerged in the sixth century B.C., antedated them by more than a century. Plato was greatly influenced by the Pythagoreans, which shows up (for example) in the *Meno*.
- No. 5: The *Meno* is the first dialogue where Plato puts words, and his own theory of knowledge, into Socrates' mouth. The famous section of the slave boy, who is shown (according to Plato) to know a special case of the Pythagorean theorem from a previous life (due to the supposed immortality of the soul), advances the notion of a divine or supernatural source of knowledge, which is the basis of Plato's theory of Forms. This means that the truth, which Plato takes to be absolute, emerges from *non*reason, from

divine intervention; which is also how he characterizes poetic inspiration. Talk about irony.

However, the real howler, or perhaps semi-howler, if we are going to be more generous, is that the primary focus of *Zen* is the Sophists, and unfortunately for Pirsig's argument, he got them (mostly) wrong. For example, while the Sophists emphasized the importance of rhetoric, they were hardly opposed to reason and rational argumentation. In fact, as several scholars have pointed out, most Athenians regarded Socrates as just another Sophist. In addition, although Socrates was opposed to rhetoric and poetry, this too was not absolute. In some of Plato's dialogues, Socrates shows both a soft spot for poetry and a respect for the Sophists, such as Protagoras of Abdera (the most famous Sophist, whose dates are 480-411 B.C.). And while it is true that overall, Plato gives the Sophists a bum rap, so to speak, the monolithic characterization of Plato vs. the Sophists, as presented by Pirsig, is overdrawn. Pirsig would have had a more convincing argument if he had taken on the whole oral-poetic tradition, which I shall turn to in Chapter 1, rather than having narrowly focused on the Sophists.

Before I do that, however, a few more words about the Sophistic movement might be in order.(4) Plato believed that persuasion, made possible through rhetoric and metaphor and poetry, were blocks to genuine knowledge. He made it his life's work to combat these, along with ethical relativism, the Sophistic notion that "Man is the measure of all things." And yet as the eminent scholar W.K.C. Guthrie points out, in the dialogue *Protagoras*, Protagoras comes off as a skilled debater, whereas Socrates is portrayed as being an unfair one. It is clear that Plato admires him, and—*mirabile dictu*—is moved by poetry as well, which is evident in the dialogue *Ion*, in which he says that the poet is "an airy thing, winged and holy." Thus Adam Nicolson, in *Why Homer Matters*, argues that Plato affects to despise poetry, but "it is clear that he was in love with it." (We tend to forget that love was a major theme in Plato's world view, as is mostly clearly evidenced in the *Symposium*.) But to give Pirsig his due, Plato does generally depict the Sophists as charlatans and tricksters, out for fame and a quick buck (or drachma)—which is something of an historical distortion.

To sum up: there is a whole list of errors in Pirsig's take on Socrates and the Sophists, except that he had the central "nugget" right: mythological thinking, or the oral-poetic tradition, was, thanks to Plato's campaign against that tradition, eventually replaced by what Pirsig calls the Church of Reason. (see n.1) This, in his view, is why modern life is so screwed up—insane, is what he argues. Let us, then, have a look at the world view that got buried.(5)

Chapter 1

The Oral-Poetic Tradition

As you set out for Ithaka
hope your road is a long one,
full of adventure, full of discovery.
Laistrygonians, Cyclops,
angry Poseidon—don't be afraid of them:
you'll never find things like that on your way
as long as you keep your thoughts raised high,
as long as a rare excitement
stirs your spirit and your body.
Laistrygonians, Cyclops,
wild Poseidon—you won't encounter them
unless you bring them along inside your soul,
unless your soul sets them up in front of you.

Hope your road is a long one.
May there be many summer mornings when,
with what pleasure, what joy,
you enter harbors you're seeing for the first time;
may you stop at Phoenician trading stations
to buy fine things,
mother of pearl and coral, amber and ebony,
sensual perfume of every kind—
as many sensual perfumes as you can;
and may you visit many Egyptian cities
to learn and go on learning from their scholars.

Keep Ithaka always in your mind.
Arriving there is what you're destined for.
But don't hurry the journey at all.
Better if it lasts for years,
so you're old by the time you reach the island,
wealthy with all you've gained on the way,
not expecting Ithaka to make you rich.

Ithaka gave you the marvelous journey.
Without her you wouldn't have set out.
She has nothing left to give you now.

And if you find her poor, Ithaka won't have fooled you.
Wise as you will have become, so full of experience,
you'll have understood by then what these Ithakas mean.
—"Ithaka," by C.P. Cavafy, trans. Edmund Keeley

> What is called oral tradition is as intricate and meaningful an art form as its derivative, "literary tradition"... [In fact], oral tradition is as "literary" as literary tradition. It is not simply a less polished, more haphazard, or cruder second cousin twice removed, to literature.
> —Albert Lord, *The Singer of Tales*

In modern Western culture, it's hard to remember that the going is the goal; or would be, if our lives made any sense. In order to do that, you have to be in touch with your body, and most of us aren't. Rationality can't help you. It's linear and abstract, and it pervades our waking lives. Constantine Cavafy, on the other hand, knew "what those Ithakas meant." He was not only one of the greatest poets of the last century; he was also among the most erotic, most sensuous poets who ever lived. Cavafy was in touch with the mimetic-mythic consciousness of his Greek ancestors, and it shines through much of his work. He employs deliberate archaisms, and makes liberal use of myth and parable. Could it be that the oral-poetic tradition survived, Plato's campaign against it notwithstanding?(1)

In order to understand this, I must ask the reader to indulge me in a brief digression regarding the evolution of human consciousness, as laid out by the psychologist Merlin Donald and the sociologist Robert Bellah. The picture is something like this:(2)

Constantine Cavafy

As far as the evolution of the brain, and cognitive development, goes, there is, says Donald, a kind of "layering phenomenon" of successive evolutionary stages, whereby the human race went from the Mimetic to the Mythic to the Theoretic. These three stages are categories of memory representation, and—the crucial point—they don't replace each other. Rather, they just accumulate. Mimesis consists of imitation and repetition, and is the basis of crafts, dance, music, and tool use. This capacity is hard-wired into the brain; it goes back four million years. The Mythic phase is also hard-wired, although it goes back only 300,000 or 400,000 years, and it consists of speech and storytelling; narrative, in a word. It includes stories of origin, legends, allegories, and so on. And finally, with Theoretic culture, we get writing systems (the first dating to 5,500 years ago, in

Mesopotamia), symbolic representation, and analysis and reflection (critical thinking, in a word). In terms of evolution, this phase is not hard-wired. It is relatively recent, and has a cultural basis rather than a biological one. As a result, its hold on us is a bit iffy, rather tenuous.

What Donald is claiming is that the modern mind is a mixture of all three of these modes, or capacities; that there was really no "replacement" of one mode of consciousness by another. For we still dance and sing, and we still tell stories, generate myths and narratives. And if our mythologies are not religious, then they are secular (modern ideologies). True, analytic thinking can do things that the other two modes can't, but these latter two "domains," says Donald, are nevertheless

> extremely subtle and powerful ways of thinking. They cannot be matched by analytic thought for intuitive speed, complexity, and shrewdness. They will continue to be crucially important in the future, because they reside in innate capacities without which human beings could not function.

Robert Bellah drives this point home with great clarity and incisiveness when he writes that narrative

> is more than [just] literature; it is the way we understand our lives. If literature merely supplied entertainment, then it wouldn't be as important as it is.

Great literature speaks to the deepest level of our humanity; it helps us better understand who we are. Narrative is not only the way we understand our personal and collective identities; it is the source of our ethics, our politics and our religion. It…isn't irrational—it can be criticized by rational argument—but it can't be derived from reason alone. *Mythic (narrative) culture is not a subset of theoretic culture, nor will it ever be. It is older than theoretic culture and remains to this day an indispensable way of relating to the world.* [Italics mine]

This is where things get tricky. If what we said in the Introduction is correct, then Donald and Bellah are wrong: there *was* a replacement of mimetic and mythic consciousness by theoretic consciousness, an operation that began with Plato. Sure, we dance and sing and tell stories and maybe do craft work and read literature (or used to), but how much of our time—most people's time—is devoted to such activities? In hard-driving capitalist societies, not very much, I would imagine. I'm also guessing that if you took a poll of Americans, asking them to say what a metaphor was, 90 percent of them would have no idea. And how many mimes/artists/poets/musicians/dancers get elected to public office? How many become CEOs of major corporations (or minor ones)? Pirsig was right: theoretic consciousness won, hands down. It's the way Western industrial and post-industrial societies and their institutions work.

And there's the rub, to jump ahead for a moment. Thinking of the oral-poetic tradition, and of bards roaming the Greek countryside (*aoidoi*, in Greek), singing the Homeric epics to enraptured audiences, Adam Nicolson writes (in *Why Homer Matters*), "this sort of rhythmic, inherited story-telling is part of the human organism." Of the body, in short, and we live in an upside-down society that is alienated from it. This is the source of our anxiety, depression, numerous addictions, and general mental illness that has reached epidemic proportions by now. The organism Nicolson speaks of is at war with itself. Who do you think is going to win?(3)

But enough digression. It is time to delineate exactly what the oral-poetic tradition was, and how it functioned in pre-literate societies. This story has, in fact, been recounted many times. Although he had a number of precursors (see below), the knockout punch (some would say deathblow) to academic classical studies was delivered by a young Harvard professor named Milman Parry (1902-35), who was able to show, with a mountain of detailed evidence, that there was no such person as Homer; that "Homer" was a name that became attached to the poems that were sung or recited by the *aoidoi* referred to above. To quote Nicolson once more, "Just as Aesop never existed but was a name around which traditional fables gathered, Homer was the name given to the poems his world composed." In a word, concludes Nicolson, "Homer" is his poetry; he is "the collective and inherited vision of great acts done long ago."(4) (More on Aesop in a moment)

Milman Parry

Before discussing the details of Parry's achievement, it should be noted that the notion of there being "many Homers" that constituted an oral tradition was not a new one. Isaac Casaubon (1559-1614), Richard Bentley (1662-1742), and Friedrich August Wolf (1759-1824) had already remarked on the fluid-like, oral nature of Homer's work. In the eighteenth century in particular, the idea was in the air that "Homer" was in fact many poets, and that the poems were the product of an entire culture. Wolf's *Prolegomena ad Homerum* (Prolegomena to Homer, 1795) argued that much of the material in the

Iliad and the *Odyssey* originally consisted of separate oral songs, and the Italian philosopher Giambattista Vico, according to Isaiah Berlin, "saw in Homer not an individual who wrote [these works], but the national genius of the Greek people itself." It is not clear whether Parry was aware of these precursors, but his entry into the field constituted a quantum leap.(5)

One thing Parry pointed out was that the function of the repetitive epithets in the Homeric epics ("rosy-fingered dawn," "swift-footed Achilles," "wine-dark sea," and so on) was not to elaborate plot or content, but rather, to maintain a *rhythm*. The epithets served to fill out lines of verse so as to "keep the great river of words flowing." These poems, he went on to say, display a different kind of creative process at work than we find in writing, but were no less creative. The repetitive nature of the oral tradition, he asserted, had a hypnotic effect, as well as a musical one. This was improv, really; jazz, if you will. Eric Havelock, in his ground-breaking study, *Preface to Plato* (more on this work below), added that the impact of the songs was highly sensual: the body was able to relax, and erotic impulses were able to come forward. The process of poetic identification, he says, meant surrendering to a spell. According to Robert Kanigel, Parry's biographer, Parry was influenced by the French anthropologist Marcel Jousse, who argued that an alternative oral truth "brought us closer to who we are as living beings than abstract squiggles on paper" (*Le style orale*, 1925). We should not be surprised that Parry was a big fan of the poetry of T.S. Eliot and e.e. cummings, where sound and rhythm are very important (one might argue that their poems are best read aloud).

So Parry believed that the repetitive nature of the oral tradition had a hypnotic effect, was sensuous, and affected the body of the listener. Robert Fitzgerald, one of his students, said that to Parry, Homer's diction "reflected a way of life, completely different from our modern days...a life which was 'holy, and sweet, and wondrous'." Media studies scholar Twyla Gibson adds:

> In a way that is difficult for literates to comprehend, what the words and phrases lost in meaning they gained in a kind of "charm" that pleased the poet and the spectators. The rhythm in the poetry became a kind of music, conveying a mood rather than a meaning, Parry asserted, and the audience became lost in the incantatory charm of the heroic.

The crux of Parry's achievement was the two trips he made to Yugoslavia during 1933-34. He and his team listened to more than 700 local bards (known as *guslari*), wrote down nearly 13,000 songs, and recorded hundreds more on 3,500 aluminum disks. These Serbo-Croatian oral epics, he discovered, shared many things in common with traditional epithets and poetic formulas. Thus Parry showed that nearly one-third of all the lines in Homer were stock phrases, and that the same pattern could be seen in the songs he recorded in the Balkans. The American historian/philosopher Walter Ong commented that Parry and his student, Albert Lord, "discovered the orality of ancient Homeric Greece not simply by studying texts but largely through sound recordings of twentieth-century Yugoslavian epic singers." Not armchair classicism, in other words, but in-the-field classicism.(6)

As an interesting aside, James Notopoulos repeated the Parry experiment with the bards of Crete in 1953, corroborating Parry's thesis.(7)

A further twist to the Homer story was provided by the British classicist Eric Havelock in 1963 with his book *Preface to Plato*, referred to above. The oral formulas, he claimed, amounted to a kind of "tribal encyclopedia," i.e., a way for the Greeks to preserve their cultural heritage. The bard, in effect, was an "encyclopedic minstrel." Poetry thus had a "storage" function, along with an educational one, of providing moral instruction. According to the Romanian professor Dumitru Tucan, it was the "central reality" of ancient Greek culture. Even during the years of Plato and Aristotle, he says, it was still the dominant voice of tradition, and of that culture. (8)

This notion of Greek epics as encyclopedias, and of poetry's purpose being one of cultural storage, was the major contribution Havelock made to Greek studies. Indeed, it has been called "revolutionary." But if his thesis is correct, it raises an interesting question. I began this chapter by arguing for the continuity of the oral-poetic tradition in the work of Constantine Cavafy, whom I regard as a direct inheritor of the mimetic-mythic mode. But why stop with Cavafy? Would it be wrong to say that a great deal of poetry falls into this category, and is thus the repository of an alternative way of being, of thinking—the alternative that Robert Pirsig was determined to restore to the center of Western life? Havelock, for his part, doesn't believe that modern poetry, which is framed in aesthetic terms, i.e., as the product of artistic inspiration, has anything in common with ancient poetry. When Plato is talking about poetry, he claims, he's not talking about our kind of poetry. If modern poetry is about inspiration and artistic creativity, he says, ancient poetry is about cultural storage. The two, he concludes, have nothing in common.

Related to this is a secondary argument, namely that Parry's research was misguided, in that (according to Havelock) his comparative method was unscientific. Ancient Greece, and twentieth-century Yugoslavia, he asserts, are worlds apart. One is of the Balkan peasantry, the other of the Homeric ruling class. Furthermore, where oral technique has survived, it is in countries where it is no longer central to their culture.

It turns out that there are experts on both sides of these arguments. For example, Princeton University's Andrew

Ford, in *Homer: The Poetry of the Past*, writes that "it is at least certain that we cannot assume a priori that such an art, answering the needs of such a different society and formed in what was to some extent a different medium, should have intuited the same values and aspired to the same effect as we see in poetry now." James Notopoulos, on the other hand, who did the Crete studies mentioned above, and whom Havelock cites, insists that "the use of memory as a means in the process of creation" is of far greater importance in oral poetry than utility. And in the course of his discussion, Havelock modifies his strict, dichotomous position, and concedes that the notion of artistic inspiration existing in ancient poetry does have some validity. He also modifies his argument regarding the Homeric ruling class, admitting that "the Homeric state of mind was...the general state of mind."(9)

Personally, I think that poetry having a storage or encyclopedic function is not necessarily at odds with it being an inspired artistic creation; from which it follows that the case for continuity would seem to have the upper hand. We can see this continuity in the work of Cavafy, as I argued in the first paragraph of this chapter. (Or in a novel such as *Zorba the Greek*, by Nikos Kazantzakis, which makes the case for body-based knowledge of reality.) In addition, I think it can be said that Cavafy's poetry also has a storage function, in terms of indirectly arguing for how we *should* live—although his incitement, for the most part, is for a personal morality, not a social one ("Waiting for the Barbarians," one of his most famous poems, would be an obvious exception). But again, why stop with Cavafy? T.S. Eliot's "Wasteland," for example, is surely an inspired achievement, and, at the same time, a catalogue or portrait of what much of Western civilization has come to—a spiritual and emotional dead end. The same might be said of Gerard Manley Hopkins' poem "God's Grandeur," or of much of the poetry of W.H. Auden. And so on.

One thing Havelock can't be faulted for, however, is his detailed elaboration of Pirsig's argument (*avant la lettre*), of how Plato managed to rout the oral-poetic tradition; to marginalize, in effect, the fundamental mode of sensual knowing. His argument goes something like this:(10)

All civilizations have an information storage system, and down to Homer, this was oral memory. Things began to change after that, and Plato was the prophet of this shift. Platonism, Havelock argues, is at bottom an appeal to substitute a conceptual discourse for an imagistic one. Book X of the *Republic* opens with an attack on poetry. Plato sees it not only as frivolous, but also as dangerous. He says it is a kind of disease, one that cripples the mind. He particularly objects to the poetic use of meter, rhythm, and harmony (Merlin Donald's Mimesis), which, he says, eclipses reason, and rouses the emotions. In effect, says Havelock, the *Republic* is a declaration of war upon the poetic experience, and it marks the introduction of the university system into the West—Pirsig's "Church of Reason." Poetry must therefore be banned from the ideal society; reason alone must be in charge. (See Section 607b of the *Republic*.)

For Plato, Havelock continues, poetry distorts reality; our salvation depends on logic. What Plato is thus searching for is a non-Homeric definition of truth, one that will replace "the rhythmically memorized flow of imagery" with the "syntax of scientific discourse." In the Homeric world view, life is experienced as a kind of dream. This explains why Book VII of the *Republic* contains the famous Parable of the Cave. By means of such a parable, Plato hopes to wake the "dreamers" up. They sit in the cave, looking at the wall, seeing the shadows cast on it by the light behind them, and taking them for reality. His goal, according to Havelock, is to get Athenians to "turn away from the panorama of sensual experience." Mimesis, mythology, the oral-poetic tradition—all of this is pathology, whereas thinking is health. That world view, that life is or should be exclusively about rationality, scientific reason, is finally anti-human, and is what is driving us crazy today—as Pirsig found out.

Occasionally some genius, like Virginia Woolf, or Ludwig Wittgenstein, makes the breakthrough, and speaks for the alternate tradition. (Regarding the shadows, Wittgenstein remarked: "Depths are on the surface."). But they are easily marginalized; individual talent is not enough to break the spell of rationality for the culture at large. So Plato did win; this much is obvious. The one exception to this victory that I can think of, starting from the early Greek context, is *Aesop's Fables*, which has had a huge cultural influence; but it is only the exception that proves the rule.

Chapter 2

The Physicality of Aesop

"sour grapes"
"crying wolf"
"a dog in the manger"
"the lion's share"
"a wolf in sheep's clothing"
—Just a few of the popular idioms derived from *Aesop's Fables*

Apparently, the *Fables* was too powerful to get marginalized. Aesop's work is still very much with us, and at the same time is clearly illustrative of non-intellectual knowing. Almost everyone has heard of him, nearly 3,000 years later; they even teach the *Fables* in school, and in 1971 Bill Cosby starred as Aesop in the TV production, "Aesop's Fables—The Tortoise and the Hare." A few words are in order, then, about its remarkable endurance record.(1)

The *Fables* has remained popular throughout history, and keeps showing up in various editions, translations, films, artworks, TV programs, and so on. In the ancient world, Aesop is mentioned by Aristotle, Aristophanes, Athenaeus, Callimachus, Lucian, Pliny, Plutarch, Seneca, and Zenobius. In the *Phaedo*, Socrates says that in his last few days, while waiting to be executed, he undertook to putting some of the *Fables* into verse form, just to relax. (There's an image for you!) Thus, says Havelock, "he reverts...to those ways of orality with which he had grown up." Apparently, he found the activity soothing.(2)

Moving forward a couple of millennia, when print was invented in the fifteenth century, the first ancient Greek work to be printed was *Aesop's Fables*. It entered English in 1484, printed by William Caxton, a merchant and diplomat. Velázquez painted a portrait of Aesop, dated 1639-40, which hangs in the Museo del Prado in Madrid, and in an illustrated Japanese edition of 1659 he is shown in Japanese dress. A comedy about him premiered at the Theatre Royal in Drury Lane, London, in 1697. Three novels were published about him in the twentieth century, and a play based on "The Fox and the Grapes" was put on in Brazil in 1953. In an American context, as we might expect, the fables "have been updated for practical business application." Titles in this genre include David Lignell, *Aesop in a Monkey Suit: Fifty Fables of the Corporate Jungle* (2006), and David

Noonan, *Aesop & the CEO: Powerful Business Insights from Aesop's Ancient Fables* (2005). The University of Illinois mounted an exhibition on Aesop in 2012 ("Wise Animals: Aesop and His Followers"), and the exhibition brochure begins with the following sentence: "No author of Greek antiquity has been more read, translated, adapted, embellished, printed, and illustrated than Aesop." Among Western authors who drew on him are La Fontaine, Jonathan Swift, Benjamin Franklin, Lessing, Emerson, Tolstoy, Robert Louis Stevenson, Oscar Wilde, James Thurber, and Alberto Moravia. Rather a star-studded lineup, I would think.

John Locke recommended the *Fables* for children; he said it would teach them how to grow up. (In fact, the Sophist Philostratus [d. ca. 247 A.D.] wrote that through the *Fables*, "children may learn the business of life.") By 1800, Aesop had become a universally approved children's author, and the *Fables* had become a staple of publishing houses that sold children's books.

There have been thousands of editions of the book, including many illustrated ones. In the nineteenth and twentieth centuries these included John Tenniel (*Alice in Wonderland*), Arthur Rackham (illustrator of Kipling, Shakespeare, Swift, et al.), Gustave Doré, and Marc Chagall.

So much for endurance; what was/is the attraction? One factor, I believe, is that the tales combine the two aspects of the oral-poetic tradition discussed in the previous chapter: they include artistic inspiration along with the "encyclopedic" function identified by Eric Havelock. But beyond that, Aesop gives us lived experience, the life of the senses, which, as J.H. Finley says (epigraph to this book), is what we all crave. The fables are not abstract or theoretical; rather, they reflect a practical and embodied philosophy. An example of embodied storytelling: At one point in his life (so the story goes), Aesop was accused of stealing figs. To prove he was innocent, he vomited; no figs came up. Vomiting is Mimetic, in Merlin Donald's sense of the term; there isn't anything Theoretical about it.

But mostly, the stories fall into the Mythic (narrative) category. They tell about life as it is, using humor, frankness, and clarity. For example, in "The Crow and the Pitcher," a crow is nearly dying with thirst, when he spies a pitcher in the distance, and flies to it. Unfortunately, it contains only a little water at the bottom; he can't reach it. So he gathers up some small pebbles lying nearby, and drops them into the pitcher, one by one. As a result, the water level slowly rises, and he is finally able to quench his thirst. Possible moral: Necessity is the mother of invention. Or maybe, Try to think outside of the box.

A second one I like is probably familiar to us all: "The Goose with the Golden Eggs." A farmer had a goose that laid a golden egg every day. But the farmer wanted the whole treasure all at once, so he killed the goose, thinking that all the eggs it contained would fall out. Unfortunately, when he opened the dead goose, it contained just what any other goose would have inside. So there would be no more golden eggs on a daily basis. The moral: Get greedy enough and it will blow up in your face.

The power of these stories lies in their direct physical simplicity, and their engaging narrative quality. The truth is acted out; it is not Theoretic, i.e., it is not analyzed via Socratic reason. You don't have to be a philosopher to get the point. "In this way," says one critic, "the fables can be regarded as similar to Greek plays and epic poetry." Aesop, if he ever existed, never wrote anything. The tales were orally transmitted, and were certainly artistically creative.

As for their "encyclopedic" function: this has generated a lot of commentary, most of which is in agreement on this point. It is clear that Aesop's stories provided a moral catalogue of his society, and they have done so down through the ages. As noted above, both Locke and Philostratus recognized their value in educating children. And not just children: the fables can be regarded as political philosophy. They tell people how they should live, and how they should live together—how to have successful social interactions. Don't cheat, don't betray others, don't be greedy, don't overreach yourself, be resourceful, be kind to others and it will pay off; and here is how to survive in a dog-eat-dog world. All of this, it seems to me, constitutes an "index" of culture, no less than the Homeric epics. So in this case at least, Plato's program of burying the oral-poetic tradition failed; Aesop managed to escape the Socratic net. Plato's image of Socrates converting the fables into poetry as he awaited death says it all.

Chapter 3

Lives of Quiet Desperation

The mass of men lead lives of quiet desperation.
—Henry David Thoreau

In 1973, Ernest Becker published *The Denial of Death*, which won the Pulitzer Prize in 1974 and became an overnight classic. In broad outline, the basic premise of the book is that human beings are afraid of death, so to hide from this knowledge, as a defense mechanism, they lay waste to the world. He was an extremely popular professor; his classes at Simon Fraser University in Vancouver were filled to overflowing. It seemed that he had astutely fingered the central problem of the human condition.

I was certainly impressed by the book; I read it more than once. But I have since come to believe that the central problem of the human condition is not the fear of death, but the fear of life. Objectively speaking, much of life is terrifying, and people want to hide from it. This means not feeling any emotions, which means living outside of one's body. A good title for that book would be *The Denial of Sense Experience*; for which, as indicated in Chapter 1, we can thank Plato. Once again, Pirsig got it right: Western reality is upside-down. Most people in the Western world can't stand to be in their own skin. They know something is terribly wrong, but they can't figure out what it is. And so, they project the problem outward; in Becker's apt phrase, they lay waste to the world or, failing that, themselves.(1)

In the mid-to-late-nineties, when I was writing *The Twilight of American Culture*, I did research documenting the coming collapse of the United States: the statistics of violence, ignorance, incompetence, mental illness, addiction, and so on. What I discovered was pretty grim; the horror is that those stats are significantly grimmer twenty-five years later. At some point after the book was published, in 2000, I stopped collecting data of that sort because what had been an impressive stream had turned into a mighty river. Who could keep up with it? I don't, as a result, have the references for these events, but anyone interested can Google the topics and find the relevant documents. In any case, consider the following:

- Massacres and mass shootings, averaging 1.1 per day. During 2015-22, more than 19,000 people were shot and killed or wounded in the US in a

mass shooting. I don't know what the figure is for 2000-2014 or 2023, but I'm guessing that if you add these in, it would at least double that number.
- In 2023, the national debt stood at more than $33 trillion, which is 123% of the nation's Gross Domestic Product.
- The endless waging of stupid, meaningless wars. Somehow, the nation is always at war, or fighting proxy wars, as in the Ukraine. Twenty wasted years in Afghanistan; the *Washington Post* did a series of front-page articles showing that no one in the government was able to say why we were there. That war also accomplished nothing at all. Here is a very astute analysis of American militarism by Jeffrey Sachs of Columbia University: https://www.commondreams.org/opinion/corruption-of-us-foreign-policy
- In 2022, the suicide rate in the US reached its highest level since 1941. Young people were especially affected.
- Depression: more than 8 percent of American adults are depressed, and 15 percent of young people are. More than 20 percent of Americans are mentally ill.
- Homicides: more than 21,000 in 2022 alone.
- Opioid addiction: more than two million Americans abuse opioids and more than ninety Americans die from opioid overdose

every day, on average. If we add to this cocaine, heroin, alcohol, and prescription drugs, the figures of addiction are through the roof.
- There is also widespread addiction to cell phones and screens. For the most part, Americans no longer read, or read very little. Or go outside.
- Widespread incidents of students attacking their teachers in class—by now, almost a commonplace. In addition, the bizarre occurrences of toddlers shooting their parents or siblings.(!)
- While adult literacy in China, Russia, and Europe is greater than 99 percent, one in five Americans is completely illiterate, and 50 percent are literate at or below the level of a sixth-grader.
- Widespread incidents of police gunning down unarmed civilians, without any provocation.
- In 2022, road rage was a factor in more than 50 percent of all car crashes that ended in fatality. In general, Americans carry a lot of anger inside themselves, just waiting to explode. "Short fuse syndrome" is also evident at fast-food establishments, where the failure to provide bacon on a cheeseburger, say, can lead (and has led) to a shooting. This has happened quite frequently.

- General callousness and lack of empathy in American life. This has been extensively documented and written about.
- Frequent articles in the press about elderly people randomly being beaten, raped, or killed, typically without a motive for the attack.
- Numerous books and articles about Americans suffering from acute loneliness.
- Possibly, the breakdown of the democratic system. In tandem with this, slowly emerging on the horizon are our opponents, or potential opponents: China, India, the Islamic states, Russia, South Africa, BRICS, and so on. We are in the midst of a tectonic change; the outcome doesn't bode well for us.
- Outright lunatics in politics: Marjorie Taylor Greene (who claimed forest fires in California were being orchestrated by "Jewish Space Lasers"), Lauren Boebert, Donald Trump, et al. At one point Sen. Lindsey Graham called upon the US to "bomb the entire world." Infestation of the political scene by conspiracy theorists such as QAnon, along with a well-documented, dramatic rise in antisemitism.
- Loss of respect for America across much of the globe. Most countries are aware that the US is on its last legs, but since it is a trigger-happy country with a huge military (something like 750 bases in eighty countries), everyone has to tiptoe around it. America has been compared to

a three-year-old toddler mindlessly waving around a bazooka.

This is really only a partial list of factors contributing to the disintegration of the US as a sociopolitical entity. For me, the country is unrecognizable from the America I knew in the 1950s. One might also argue that it is unrecognizable from what it was thirty years ago. I predicted the collapse of the country in *The Twilight of American Culture* (2000). Since then, people have written me to ask when that was going to happen. My answer is always the same: "What do you think is going on right now? Just look around!" But I do believe a severe crash, worse than the one of 2008, is in the pipeline for us, and that by 2030, America will effectively be "over," a cardboard cutout of its former self. Like England: irrelevant, maybe even worse.

Clearly, we have entered a period of national dementia. Freud once wrote that it was possible for an entire civilization to be neurotic, but I think we can now say that "psychotic" would be a more accurate description. Freud's concept of the Death Instinct (Thanatos) is also applicable to contemporary America. We are thrashing around, in our death throes, and the rest of the world knows it. Nemesis: whom the gods wish to destroy, the saying goes, they first drive insane.

Of course, not all of this can be attributed to the Platonic takeover of Western consciousness, but I do believe the connection is there. Cut off from the oral-poetic tradition, from grounded sense experience, our lives have no meaning, and this is driving us around the bend. Granted, the *Iliad* is about war, and it's a pretty brutal epic. And the *Odyssey* is about a man on a long journey, trying to return to Ithaka, i.e., to find himself. But the larger context of Homeric society is one of bards singing tales to audiences who are living out a mythology they can believe in, and this is something that post-Socratic culture wound up losing. As Pirsig, Havelock, and many other writers have pointed out, we are the inheritors of that loss, and as a result we are at a loss as to how to live, what to do with our lives. The statistics quoted above make that perfectly clear, it seems to me.

The "Pirsig Project," as it were, is of course itself insane; if reality got turned upside-down 2,500 years ago, it isn't likely that we can get society back upright, so to speak, and certainly not any time soon (if ever). For let's not kid ourselves: tectonic changes take time. The last one of this magnitude was the shift from medieval to modern, which was a gradual process; it took two centuries to effect. The great chronicler of that shift was the Dutch historian Johan Huizinga, in his classic work, *The Waning of the Middle Ages*. The book showed that those two centuries were ones of widespread pessimism and psychological depression, because as the Middle Ages disintegrated, people lost their moorings, the sense of who they were, and what their place was in the larger society. (The Black Death—bubonic plague—of the mid-fourteenth century didn't help, of course; and we in the twenty-first century have had our own milder version of it.)(2)

In terms of reconnecting with our bodies, there are many brilliant guides around: *Depression and the Body*, for example (Alexander Lowen), or *The Body Keeps the Score* (Bessel van der Kolk). The problem is that all of the books in this genre are concerned with *individual* healing and recovery; they cannot seriously speak to the larger social, cultural, economic, and political issues. Where, indeed, would one begin? Declare a National Cavafy Day? No, the reality is that things will probably go on as they are, and in the foreseeable future they are likely to get worse. The "vector of history," so to speak, has to play itself out, and it won't be pretty. All one can hope for is that on the other side of that watershed, there will be some recovery of the oral-poetic tradition, of a sensual relationship to the world, of meaning and true spirituality, and that healing will be part of our destiny. Who knows? Maybe Robert Pirsig will have the last laugh, after all.

Chapter 4

Backlash

Hope is nostalgia for the future.
—Anonymous

One thing that was in vogue a few years ago was the appearance of self-contradictory books about America's future. A number of monographs followed this curious formula: in a book of, say, 300 pages, 290 of them would constitute a careful documentation of the inevitable collapse of the American empire. Then suddenly, the author did an unexpected *volte face*, and in the final ten pages or so told his readers how that collapse could be, and even would be, avoided. It was like a magician pulling a rabbit out of a hat at the last minute. What had apparently happened was that the author was not able to face up to the conclusion that logically followed from his data, so he went into denial mode, or maybe we should call it false-optimism mode. Reader, rest assured, what you have before you is not that kind of book. I do believe things will eventually get better, because I (naively?) believe in the enduring quality of the human spirit. So for the most part, when I talk about future possibilities, I am referring to post-breakdown ones. Things will get a lot worse before they improve.

Writing in *The Guardian* on 28 December 2023, someone named Ross Barkan predicted that there would be a backlash against the techno-rational society. Young people in particular were throwing away their smartphones and turning instead to things such as astrology. "The zeitgeist is changing," he declares. "A strange, romantic backlash to the tech era looms. Empiricism, algorithms and smartphones are out—astrology, art and a life lived fiercely offline are in." In Japan, they call these "dropouts" from mainstream society the "Satori Generation"; they constitute about 1 percent of the population. Something similar is happening in Italy. *Ojala!* I am tempted to say; if only.(1)

Many years ago, in my Assistant Professor days, I remember talking with an older colleague about how spiritual or emotional energy manifested in various societies. He said something I never forgot. "Look," he told me, "there are two types of barbarism. One is a society in which everything is rational, and another in which everything is irrational." Given what I have written up to this point, I think it's safe to say that current Western barbarism falls into the first category.

Nietzsche was hoping for a reconciliation between Apollo and Dionysus; so was Robert Pirsig. Thus he writes in *Zen*: "What has become an urgent necessity is a way of looking at the world that does violence to neither of these two kinds of understanding and unites them into one."(2)

In that spirit, I'd like to conclude this book by speculating about post-breakdown possibilities: post-2040, let's say, or maybe even post-2050. "Nostalgia for the future," writes the journalist Robert Camuto, "means taking the lessons and the good of the past and carrying them forward with a vision of tomorrow."(3) The image I have in mind is that of a spiral rather than a circle. Clearly, Western societies can't return to square one; no sane person would want that, in any case. But if we can draw on the positive ideas and institutions of the past, we in effect return to square one, but at a higher level. (The poet Gary Snyder once said to me that his own image of this reparation project was one of "rummaging about in the used parts bin." That also works, I'm guessing, although in the list below we are talking more about subtracting rather than adding.) My list is as follows:

1. Secession of various parts of the US into smaller states or regions
2. Rejection of a good deal of hi-tech communications technology
3. What I have referred to elsewhere as Dual Process

4. Revival of the "kinship world view," in particular, Native American ways of life
5. Mass rejection of consumerism
6. Mass resignation from stupid, monotonous jobs; the "Satori Switch"

Yes, much of this is utopian, not really feasible; but I have a feeling that in the wake of the coming crash/collapse/breakdown, these options may suddenly acquire great appeal. In any case, let's take a closer look at them.

Secession(4)

As a number of historians have indicated, the desire for secession, or separatism, was present in America almost as soon as the ink dried on the Constitution. America's union, according to historian and journalist Richard Kreitner, was quite imperfect. The "seduction" of secession was present at the beginning and has never gone away. Some of these historians have even wondered why the Civil War took so long to occur.

When I began to research recent secessionist movements, say, from the 1980s to today, I discovered quite a list. There were lots of such movements, and most of them still exist; but all of the efforts to create new states or regions have, up to this point, failed. Which is to be expected. If, for example, Vermont, which has a strong secessionist movement, were to suddenly declare its independence from the rest of the US, the Marines would be on the streets of Burlington in less than two hours. But as the American military gets weaker and weaker (which has been very well documented), there may come a time when the federal government doesn't have the resources, or the will, to prevent something like that from happening. This will seem far-fetched until it actually occurs.

In any case, here is a list of a few secessionist movements by state:

- Alaska: the Alaska Independence Party
- California: the California National Party
- Hawaii: the Hawaiian Sovereignty Movement
- New Hampshire: the New Hampshire Liberty Party, and the Free State Project
- South Carolina: the Third Palmetto Republic
- Texas: the Republic of Texas, and the Texas Nationalist Movement
- Vermont: the Second Vermont Republic

And here, a list of several movements by region:

- American Redoubt: Idaho, Montana, Wyoming, and parts of Oregon and Washington
- Republic of Lakotah: by the Lakota people
- Pacific Northwest: Cascadia: Washington, Oregon, part of British Columbia, and possibly parts of Northern California, Southern Alaska, Idaho, and Western Montana

- Deseret: Utah, Mormon "theodemocracy"
- League of the South: former Confederate States of America
- Northwest Territorial Imperative
- Aztlán: Chicano nation
- Republic of New Afrika: black separatists

How far-fetched is all this, really? A Zogby International poll of 2017 revealed that 68 percent of Americans were open to the notion of secession.

All of this raises the question of what the benefits of secession might be. A major one, to my mind, would be that the resulting states or regions would be too small, and/or insufficiently wealthy, to make war. Empires can make war; decentralized sections of the US (or of Russia, for that matter), would be hard put to do so. The well-documented horror visited upon the world by the American empire would hopefully be a thing of the past. Ronald Reagan labeled the Soviet Union "the evil empire," and he was right. He just conveniently forgot to mention that America could also be characterized by a similar label.(5)

F.H. Buckley, a law professor at George Mason University, in his book *American Secession*, notes that smaller countries enjoy less militarism; are happier, and less corrupt; and are a lot freer. And to my mind, Ernest Callenbach's beautiful book of 1975, *Ecotopia*—which places a heavy emphasis on protecting the environment —makes a very good case for the benefits of secession, and was understandably a best-seller for many years. It also made a pitch for more eros, greater sensuality, and greater embodiment, although he doesn't refer to the oral-poetic tradition per se.

Callenbach died in 2012, and shortly after that his literary agent discovered an unpublished essay in his computer files. It was apparently the last thing he wrote. The ending of the essay reads as follows:

> All things "go" somewhere: they evolve, with or without us, into new forms. So as the decades pass, we should try not always to futilely fight these transformations....We can embrace this process of devolution: embellish it when strength avails, learn to love it....Let us embrace decay, for it is the source of all new life and growth.(6)

Things falling apart, in other words, may be not only inevitable, but also beneficial. We may need to start thinking of secession in a positive light.

There will, of course, be a lot of strong disagreements with what I have just written. Secession is surely a controversial topic. But as a future option for a post-collapsed world, I believe it warrants an extended discussion.

Rejection of Technology

Of all the items on the above list, this one comes closest to a revival of the oral-poetic tradition, because it would mean undercutting the dominance that science and rationality have over our lives. Of course, I am not talking about a rejection of *all* technology, or of all science and rationality. No one wants that, and it would be impossible in any case. The goal is not abolition, but rebalancing, so to speak, for we are grossly out of balance. In this regard, the *Guardian* article by Ross Barkan, cited above, deserves some serious attention. He is describing a revulsion, mostly on the part of young people, toward the hi-tech world we are forced to swim in, and their attempts to free themselves from it. Consciously or not, they understand that a culture so heavily defined by technology and scientific rationalism is making people sick. It has no spiritual content, and at the end of the day, it renders our lives meaningless.

The abstraction of life began with the Scientific Revolution of the seventeenth century, and has accelerated ever since, being identified with "progress." As Octavio Paz once remarked, we sorely need a new definition of "progress." The promise of science, technology, and rationality in general was that under the aegis of these things, life would get better. According to Barkan, young people, at least, are beginning to see this as hype. "The new romantics," he says, "wonder: what good has any of this done for us? Were hyper-sophisticated GPS devices, cameras and video recorders worth it?" For what is obvious is that life has gotten demonstrably *worse* over the last twenty years; it hardly takes a genius to see that. Two decades of digital technology have reduced our lives to kitsch, and now Artificial Intelligence—AI—threatens to make those lives even kitschier. Barkan terms all of this technology "rapacious."

As an example, let me address just one bit of the new technology of the last twenty years, namely cell phones. I finally stopped collecting the references and citations for this, because they began to accumulate quite heavily over the last few years, and I felt: OK, OK, I get the message. What these books and articles increasingly began to document was how destructive, and self-destructive, this technology was. In a word: cell phones and smartphones have significantly increased the amount of anxiety and depression Americans are experiencing (especially young Americans). They keep us on call, and also (de facto) working, 24/7. They make it impossible to be alone, or to be left alone; to have creative quiet time, to read or to meditate. There is even some evidence that they make us dumber, and affect the physiology of the brain. And they cut us off from the direct experience of nature, of the real world. In his novel *The Circle*, Dave Eggers gives us a grim picture of a future dystopian life, completely dominated by communications technology. And Gary Shteyngart, in *Super Sad True Love Story*, imagines a situation in which the ethernet breaks down, such that cell phones have no more use than paper weights, and in which people don't know what to do with themselves because they have lost the ability to read. It is interesting to note that decades before Eggers or Shteyngart, the historian Daniel Boorstin, who was later to become the Librarian of Congress, predicted much of this, especially the issue of not being present in the real world. We swim in "simulacra," he wrote, living at one remove from reality.)(7)

However, it is my sad duty to report to you that mass rejection or abandonment of this technology is, unfortunately, not a likely prospect, because people are typically addicted to their phones. It is a case of technology using them, rather than of them using technology—an old theme of many science fiction novels. In Chapter 3 of my book *Why America Failed*, I document the intense hold that technology has over Americans, at least since the Erie Canal of 1825, such that it really amounts to America's hidden religion. Which is why if you ask someone nearby, who is loudly talking into his or her phone, to please take the conversation somewhere else, you are typically met with incredible rage, and are likely to find yourself in the midst of a major fight.(8)

All of this has serious international implications as well. A recent article (7 December 2023) by Nicolas Niarchos in the *New York Review of Books* consists of a review of five books on cobalt mining in the Congo—cobalt being the essential mineral used in cell phones—and how our use of these phones makes possible the brutality of the mining industry. (Among other things, the mining of exotic minerals exposes the miners to toxic vapors, thereby shortening their lives.) The lead book under review is by Siddharth Kara, *Cobalt Red: How the Blood of the Congo Powers Our Lives*. Kara's study documents things such as child labor, exposure to toxic chemicals, wage slavery, tunnel collapse (killing huge numbers of workers), and the high rate of rape, among other atrocities. (I remember reading, several months ago, an article about the rape of an eighteen-month-old baby in the mines.) Kara writes that we finally have to face up to the "blood-for-cobalt economy." Niarchos adds, "I can attest to just how shocking the conditions in some mines are-- and even more so considering that the minerals will end up in the devices that are so much a part of our daily lives." Apparently, butchery in the Global South is OK, inasmuch as it makes life in the Global North a bit more "convenient." In a word, the Global North doesn't give a damn.(9)

Amnesty International did a report on all of this much earlier, in 2016, entitled "This Is What We Die For." In addition, much of this was anticipated by the actress Robin Wright, who has been conducting a campaign against the use of these phones since 2011. CNN reported this effort under the title "Your Cell Phone, Congo's Misery," which article also discussed the release of a documentary entitled "Blood in the Mobile."(10)

Alan Turing

To switch gears, in conclusion: a very revealing instance of the digital takeover of genuine spirituality and embodiment is the case of the British mathematician and computer scientist, Alan Turing (1912-54), whose work made possible the field of Artificial Intelligence. He was the doyen of digital technology, asserting that any human behavior or characteristic could be duplicated by a machine. Yet at age twenty-two, during Christmas of 1934, he asked for, and got, a teddy bear. He said he had never had one as a little boy. If we turn to the work of psychoanalyst and pediatrician Donald Winnicott on "Transitional Objects," it suggests that on some level, Turing understood that something primal was missing from his life, and that he was attempting to fill the void with computers and calculation. In effect, computers, and the idea of a mechanized society, became his Transitional Object. The addiction of millions of people today to screens, smartphones, and other digital devices are a repetition of that sad psychological process, whereby our spiritual lives are channeled into mechanism, or virtual reality.

In any case, toward the end of his life Turing seemed to dimly understand that he had been living a kind of synthetic existence, and became interested in the spiritual dimension of life he had repressed long ago. So he began seeing a Jungian analyst, and started reading Tolstoy and E.M. Forster, champions of the inner life. One cannot know for sure, but it seems likely that this late interest in "soul-writers" like Jung et al. was a source of emotional expansion for him; that he was finally opening the door to a real life as opposed to a digital substitute. A sensory life, one might say; perhaps even an oral-poetic one.(11)

One can only hope that the "romantic rebellion" against all of this destructive technology reported by Ross Barkan will turn into a major political movement, but at this point, he writes, "Facebook, Apple, Amazon and Google are hegemonic"; and as for Mark Zuckerberg (who comes across as strangely robotic), "He and his ilk own the present." No, this is not "progress" in any meaningful sense of the term. In effect, cell phone addiction and its attendant technologies have usurped the possibility of a grounded way of life—at least for now.

Dual Process

What I refer to as Dual Process is one item on the list above that is not post-collapse; it needs to happen right now. As the institutions of capitalism continue to disintegrate, we—whoever that is—need to be constructing new replacement institutions along the lines of an alternative model to capitalism. As the biologist David Ehrenfeld has written, "Our first task is to create a shadow economic, social, and even technological structure that will be ready to take over as the existing system fails." That capitalism will be pretty much finished by the year 2100 is more than likely, and I provide detailed data for this argument in my essay of several years ago on Dual Process. So the first part of the process is the disintegration; the second part is the replacement. In what follows, I intend to concentrate on the latter. What might some of these alternatives consist of?(12)

For example: as of 2012 there were no less than 325 alternative currency experiments operating in Spain, barter included, and I'm guessing that figure must be much higher today. Barcelona, it turns out, has more than 100 "time banks" involving thousands of customers, that allow people to trade services without the use of money —what has been called a "parallel economy." Meanwhile, the most dramatic success story in Spain in recent times is that of the town of Marinaleda, in Andalucía, as told by Dan Hancox in *The Village Against the World*. The town has (or had) 2,700 people, and for thirty years (as of twenty years ago) its citizens employed hunger strikes and demonstrations to achieve the type of society they wanted, a society in which everyone had a job and a home. Profits from enterprises such as the olive oil cooperative were plowed back into the village. The inhabitants built their own homes; mortgage payments were fifteen euros a month. Protests, and clashes with the police, went on for years. In 1991, 1,200 hectares were expropriated from the Duke of Infantado and made into an agricultural co-op for root crops and olive groves. Moral of the story: it isn't easy to break with the dominant (expansionist) culture, but on the local level, at least, it's not impossible.

Moving on from Spain: Japan is the country that has more of what are called "complementary currency" programs—more than 600 of them—than any other country in the world. Essentially, these are agreements within a community to accept something other than legal tender as a means of payment. They don't replace the yen; they just run parallel to it as a kind of barter system. The domestic solar power market in Japan reached something like 20 billion US dollars in 2013; and the nation's "ecological footprint," defined as the per person resource demand, is comparatively light. Whereas the United States placed fifth-highest on the list of the Global Footprint Network for 2007, Japan ranked thirty-sixth.

The huge popularity of Kohei Saito's recent book, *Capital in the Anthropocene* (quick sales of half a million copies, mostly purchased by Japanese youth), is another indicator of tendencies in a Dual Process direction (Saito has been hailed as the "Green Marx"). Saito has joined with other environmental activists to create the Common Forest Foundation, which purchased land around Mount Takao near Tokyo to save the "public good" of forested areas from commercial development. (13)

By now the reader will have noticed that I have omitted the US from this discussion of Dual Process. That is because I don't think it has much of a chance of succeeding in America; it is far more likely to take hold in Europe, Latin America, and Japan. The reason for this is that the (anti-)spiritual tradition of the North American continent, for more than 400 years now, is that of hustling, competition. Plainly put, Americans don't really know how to work together, how to get along with others. If two American men meet, for example, rather than viewing the other person as a potential friend, each regards the other as a potential rival. It's a crummy way to live, but that is the reigning ideology. The political scientist and environmental pioneer, William Ophuls, who served as assistant to several US ambassadors to Japan, captured it exactly in his article of 1974, "The Economy vs. the Environment":

> I don't really think that Americans as a whole are capable of facing up to these hard choices and making [these] kind[s] of self-disciplined policies and

imposing them on themselves. I guess I can say this in part because I have experience in Japan where, even in a modern age with a relatively free market economic system, they still remain extraordinarily communalistic. I suspect the Japanese would adapt rather well to a stationary state economy.

The defining characteristic of Japanese consciousness, in fact, is that of working together, group mentality (which has both positive and negative aspects, of course).(14) Americans don't have a minimalist tradition, and they are not wired up for Buddhism, restraint, communal life, or limits to growth, and quite frankly, I doubt there is a more narcissistic, self-involved collection of people on the planet. When the crunch comes, or even as it is already coming down, the chances are that the US will descend into chaos and martial law. A steady-state economy is simply unimaginable to Americans, who have been nurtured for centuries on the notion of an endless frontier of unlimited goods and energy—the American Dream. They thus lack the historical background, or emotional resources, to adapt to such a way of life. Sokei-an, America's first Zen master (d. 1945), wrote that introducing Buddhism to Americans was like "holding a lotus to a rock and hoping it will take root." At the end of the day (or decade), the rock is still a rock, because the American way of life consists of outperforming the next guy, showing that you are better than him or everyone else. Most Americans regard such behavior as admirable, sensible, and simply "the way of the world." There is a word for such people: fools.

Revival of the Kinship World View

For reasons just stated, this possibility doesn't have much chance of taking hold in the United States. It can only spread in those countries that don't have such a strong individualistic, and competitive, ideology as the US, and where there is a thriving environmental movement. As far as America goes, however, the last few decades have seen the publication of numerous books admiring Native American ways of life, and arguing for the necessity of emulating those ways—"shifting paradigms" is the popular phrase—so as to save the planet, turn things around. Of course, in terms of climate change and sustainability, things have only gotten worse, planet-wise, in the intervening years. The 2015 Paris climate agreement, for example, was inspiring, but as it had no means of punishing those nations that violated the agreement, it was, in retrospect, just a piece of theater. It made the participants feel good, but it had no teeth.

This raises the crucial question of No matter how sane the indigenous world view is, how do these writers propose to implement it? For the same thing can be said about the fleet of environmental books published during the Carter administration, and of Jimmy's heartfelt effort to change things (including the

American passion for consumerism). All of this was blown away by Ronald Reagan's landslide election in 1980, and his subsequent reaffirmation of the dominant capitalist paradigm/American Dream. The vote made it clear that the American people had very little interest in President Carter's call for sustainability and restraint, and a great interest in buying things, and in pursuing individual "success." I'm guessing that most of those optimistic books are now out of print, or buried on the shelves of used bookstores. In a word, calls for change are not the same thing as actual change.

In any case, the latest comer in the field is *Restoring the Kinship Worldview*, by Wahinkpe Topa (Four Arrows) and Darcia Narvaez, 2022. It's a lovely book, drawing on twenty-eight indigenous voices to explain or explore the Native American world view, which is one of kinship rather than competition. The opening pages contain a large number of endorsements, all affirming the need to shift the American mindset from exploitation of the earth to seeing ourselves as one with the earth. Only one of these blurbs (or twenty-eight essays) hints at the problem of how to effect this monumental shift: mine. I say that the alternative voice needs to be heard, but add what I regard as the crucial question: "Is anyone listening?" The obvious answer is, Very few. Reaganism is still the order of the day. No one in this book takes on the central issue, namely how to implement this proposed shift in consciousness. Once again, just stating the need for this shift won't generate a shift. If it would, it would have happened long ago.(15)

As a result, and regrettably, this section of Chapter 4 has to be rather short.

Rejection of Consumerism

Ditto. The frenzy for shopping is an attempt on the part of consumers to fill the emptiness in their lives, the Void at the center of their souls. If they were embodied and fulfilled, this wouldn't be going on. I don't imagine that a change in this state of affairs is going to happen any time soon. To quote from the Native American tradition discussed above, "The love of possessions is a disease with them." (Sitting Bull, 1877). (16)

Quitting Meaningless Jobs

This has actually gone beyond the level of individual decisions. Of Americans in Generation Z—i.e., born in the late 1990s and early 2000s—73% say a healthy work-life balance is more important than salary. Millennials are also quitting in droves because they find their jobs meaningless. There have, in recent years, been numerous articles on the subject in a variety of magazines, including avowedly capitalist ones like *Forbes*. It seems to have turned into something of a political movement, going by names such as "The Great Resignation," or "The YOLO Economy" (You Only Live

Once). The trend is not limited to America, and also cuts across the entire socioeconomic spectrum. Anne Helen Petersen, who edits the *Culture Study* newsletter, in her article "From Burnout to Radicalization," tells her readers that "Career was my identity. Now I realize it's all a capitalist scam." (She is also the author of *Can't Even: How Millennials Became the Burnout Generation*.) She's not the only one coming to that conclusion. And it's a conclusion that flies in the face of the Protestant Ethic and the American Dream: work hard and you'll get ahead. Just as we need to redefine "progress," so we need to redefine "success," because professional or career ambition doesn't cut it any more for a lot of people.

Of course, if it is really to become a political movement, we need to ask How many people? And: What about those people who can't afford to quit? "The question," writes Sarah Todd in *Quartz* magazine, "is whether individual white-collar workers quitting their jobs could add up to a bigger paradigm shift." In order for that to happen, the personal has to become political, as the once-popular saying goes. As it turns out, in 2021, forty-seven million American workers quit their jobs. At this point, it is hard to say what all of this amounts to. One can only hope.(17)

In conclusion, let me say that this summary does not exhaust the list of alternative possibilities that you, the reader, can probably think of. As for me, my hope is that changes of this sort might enable us to reconnect with our senses, with the sensory reality of the world, and even possibly, with the oral-poetic tradition. As I said earlier, the image is that of a helix. We cannot return to pre-Socratic days, and we can't, à la Pirsig, defeat Reason on its own turf. But we just may be able to recapture something of what we have lost, and that, I believe, has become a matter of dire necessity. Once again: *Ojala!*

Notes

Introduction

1. Another example of Pirsig's thesis about the ancient Greeks (discussed below) being in the air around this time is the publication of *Vom Mythos zum Logos* (From Mythos to Logos, or From Myth to Reason), by the German philosopher Wilhelm Nestle, one year after the publication of *Zen*. I don't know if Nestle read English or, if he did, if he had read Pirsig's work; but it doesn't really matter all that much, his book being part of the zeitgeist. The purpose of my book, wrote Nestle, is to show "the progressive replacement of mythological by rational thinking among the Greeks." Good Pirsigism, so to speak.
2. Friedrich Nietzsche, *The Birth of Tragedy*, trans. Walter Kaufman (New York: Doubleday Anchor, 1956; orig. German ed. 1872), pp. 84-85, 94, and 137.
3. J.H. Finley, *Four Stages of Greek Thought* (Stanford: Stanford University Press, 1966), pp. 102 and 105; Robert Pirsig, *Zen and the Art of Motorcycle Maintenance* (New York: William Morrow, 1974), pp. 84, 91, and 117. Pirsig can hardly be dismissed as some sort of anti-academic oddball (or zealot). Consider the following observation by John Gray in his latest work, *The New Leviathans*: "Imagining that abstractions conjured up by language were independently existing realities, [Plato and Aristotle] led the human mind into millennia of feeble self-deception." I would substitute "powerful" for "feeble," however. (Quoted in the review of Gray by John Banville in the *New York Review of Books*, 21 December 2023, pp. 82-83.)
4. The following discussion is based on a number of sources: W.K.C. Guthrie, *The Greek Philosophers* (New York: Harper & Row, 1960), p. 71; Philip Wheelwright, *The Presocratics* (Odyssey Press, 1966), p. 238; *Protagoras*, trans. W.K.C. Guthrie (New York: Penguin Books, 1956), pp. 21-22; Jonathan Lavilla de Lera and Javier Aguirre Santos, "The Philosopher against the Rhapsodist," *Filozofia*, vol. 72 no. 2 (2018),

pp. 108-18; Adam Nicolson, *Why Homer Matters* (New York: Picador, 2014), p. 33; and "The Sophists," *Stanford Encyclopedia of Philosophy*.
5. Pirsig's take on modern life has obvious echoes with the work of the Scottish psychiatrist R.D. Laing, who also argued that reality was inverted (psychotics were sane, and ordinary people, including society at large, were insane), and who was also lionized as a guru by millions of readers. Laing's thesis was first presented in *The Divided Self* (1960), and followed up in a series of widely read monographs. The notion of inversion is a stark, highly controversial, and dramatic statement, and it put both men on the map. Both of them became "culture-bearers" as a result.

CHAPTER ONE

1. Robert Liddell, *Cavafy* (New York: Pocket Books, 1974), pp. 12 and 136.
2. In the discussion that follows I am borrowing liberally from Appendix III of my book *Neurotic Beauty* (Healdsburg CA: Water Street Press, 2019).
3. Adam Nicolson, *Why Homer Matters* (New York: Picador, 2014), p. 83.
4. Ibid., p. 54; Adam Kirsch, "The Echoing Song," *New Yorker*, 14 June 2021, pp. 72-75.
5. Nicolson, *Why Homer Matters*, p. 40; "Homer" and "Homeric Question," Wikipedia; Isaiah Berlin, *Vico and Herder* (New York: Viking, 1976), p. 55. The discussion that follows is taken from my *Eminent Post-Victorians* (Independent Publication, 2022), pp. 32-34; Robert Kanigel, *Hearing Homer's Song* (New York: Knopf, 2021), passim; Eric Havelock, *Preface to Plato* (Cambridge MA: Belknap Press, 1963), pp. 29, 89, 147, 152, and 207; and Twyla Gibson, "Milman Parry: The Oral-Formulaic Style of the Homeric Tradition," at McLuhan Program - Toronto School of Communications - Milman Parry (archive.org).
6. Nicolson, *Why Homer Matters*, pp. 77, 83, and 86; "Homer," Wikipedia; Walter Ong, "Literacy and Orality in Our Times," *Journal of Communication*, vol. 30 no. 1 (March 1980), pp. 197-204. Somewhere I read that the material Parry collected, and subsequently deposited in the Harvard library, actually weighed a ton(!); but I have lost the reference.

7. James Notopoulos, "The Genesis of an Oral Heroic Poem," *Greek, Roman, and Byzantine Studies*, vol. 3 no. 2/3 (1960).
8. Havelock, *Preface to Plato*, pp. 29, 83, and 89; Dumitru Tucan, "The quarrel between poetry and philosophy," *Procedia, 71* (2013), pp. 168-75. On the following discussion see Havelock, pp. 43 and 93-94.
9. Andrew Ford, *Homer: The Poetry of the Past* (Ithaca NY: Cornell University Press, 2019), p. 2; Havelock, *Preface to Plato*, pp. 93, 94 n.8, and 134-35.
10. The discussion that follows is taken from *Preface to Plato*, pp. viii, 3-4, 15, 26, 47, 91, 182, 190, 205, 239, and 254.

Chapter Two

1. On Cosby: "Aesop," Wikipedia. Sources for the following discussion also include "AESOP—ANCIENT GREECE—CLASSICAL LITERATURE," https://ancient-literature.com/greece_aesop/ ; Edward Clayton, "Aesop's Fables," Internet Encyclopedia of Philosophy; "Wise Animals: Aesop and His Followers," Exhibition at the University of Illinois, 2012, cooper.library.illinois.edu/rbx/exhibitions/Aesop/aesop-life.html; "Aesop's Fables," https://www.umass.edu/aesop/history/php; and Jack Zipes (ed.), *Aesop's Fables* (New York: Signet Classics, 1992), with an Introduction by Sam Pickering and an Afterword by Jack Zipes (the book contains 203 fables).
2. Eric Havelock, *The Muse Learns to Write* (New Haven: Yale University Press, 1986), p. 116.

Chapter Three

1. Ernest Becker, *The Denial of Death* (Los Angeles: Free Press, 1973); see also Morris Berman, *Healing: The Defining Root of Our Existence* (Independent Publication, 2023).
2. "Johan Huizinga," Wikipedia; Johan Huizinga, *The Waning of the Middle Ages* (New York: Dover, 2013; orig. Dutch ed. 1919).

Chapter Four

1. The zeitgeist is changing. A strange, romantic backlash to the tech era looms | Ross Barkan | The Guardian. The "Satori Generation" has withdrawn from high-paying corporate jobs and relocated to the countryside, fishing, making jam, etc. As for Italy, see Back to the land: young Italians find la dolce vita in a return to farming | Global development | The Guardian.
2. Robert Pirsig, *Zen and the Art of Motorcycle Maintenance* (New York: William Morrow, 1974), p. 83.
3. Robert Camuto, "Getting nostalgic for the *future*," at Getting nostalgic for the future - Robert Camuto author.
4. Sources for the following discussion include "Secession in the United States," Wikipedia; Richard Kreitner, *Break It Up* (Boston: Little, Brown and Company, 2020); and F.H. Buckley, *American Secession* (New York: Encounter Books, 2020).
5. The literature on what the US has visited upon the world is quite huge. Luckily for the US government, almost all of the American population doesn't care, or prefers to remain ignorant. Those interested in pursuing this issue, however, might consult the following items, for starters: Norman Solomon, *War Made Invisible: How America Hides the Human Toll of Its Military Machine* (New York: New Press, 2023); Nick Turse, *Kill Anything That Moves: The Real American War in Vietnam* (New York: Metropolitan Books, 2013); Bevan Hurley, "From Cambodia to Bangladesh: a brief history of Henry Kissinger's alleged war crimes," *The Independent* (London), 3 December 2023: "Henry Kissinger sided with military dictators and genocidal regimes in his pursuit of projecting US power during the Cold War, resulting in the deaths of millions of innocents."
6. I quote Callenbach on pp. 181-82 of *Are We There Yet?* (Brattleboro VT: Echo Point Books, 2017).
7. Daniel Boorstin, *The Image: A Guide to Pseudo-Events in America* (New York: Vintage, 1992; orig. publ. 1961).
8. Morris Berman, *Why America Failed: The Roots of Imperial Decline* (New York: John Wiley and Sons, 2011), Chapter 3.
9. Nicolas Niarchos, "In Congo's Cobalt Mines," *New York Review of Books*, 7 December 2023.

10. Robin Wright on CNN: Your Cell Phone, Congo's Misery - The Enough Project
11. On Turing see my *Eminent Post-Victorians* (Independent Publication, 2022), pp. 108-19.
12. Morris Berman, "Dual Process: The Only Game in Town," in *Are We There Yet?*, pp. 205-17. For the discussion that follows I am drawing on the concluding chapter of my *Neurotic Beauty* (Healdsburg CA: Water Street Press, 2019).
13. Nathan Gardels, "Degrowth in Japan," Degrowth In Japan - NOEMA (noemamag.com), 5 May 2023; Kohei Saito, *Capital in the Anthropocene* (Cambridge: Cambridge University Press, 2023, reprint edition).
14. On Japanese group mentality see the discussion in *Neurotic Beauty* (above, n.12) and also the classic work by Takeo Doi, *The Anatomy of Dependence*. In Japanese, this concept is known as *amae*.
15. Wahinkpe Topa (Four Arrows) and Darcia Narvaez, *Restoring the Kinship Worldview* (Berkeley CA: North Atlantic Books, 2022). For a concrete, no-nonsense view of how to try to make the shift, I recommend a movie called *The East*: The East (2013 film) - Wikipedia.
16. For a humorous take on this possibility, see the second story in my short story collection, *The Heart of the Matter* (Brattleboro VT: Echo Point Books, 2020), and also my novel, *The Man Without Qualities* (New York: Oliver Arts and Open Press, 2016).
17. Quitting your job is now a political act (qz.com), and André Gorz Was the Theorist Who Predicted the Revolt Against Meaningless Work (jacobin.com). See also Nicole Aschoff, *The New Prophets of Capital* (London: Verso Books, 2015).

About the Author

Morris Berman is a poet, novelist, essayist, social critic, and cultural historian. He has written twenty books and nearly 200 articles, and has taught at a number of universities in Europe, North America, and Mexico. He won the Governor's Writers Award for Washington State in 1990, and was the first recipient of the annual Rollo May Center Grant for Humanistic Studies in 1992. In 2000, *The Twilight of American Culture* was named a "Notable Book" by the *New York Times Book Review*, and in 2013 he received the Neil Postman Award for Career Achievement in Public Intellectual Activity from the Media Ecology Association. Dr. Berman lives in Mexico.

Printed in Dunstable, United Kingdom